My Connemara

Joyce Country

Amelia Joyce

A Connemara Guidebook

Paperback edition first published 2018 by Book Hub Publishing, Ireland.
Revised 2nd edition published 2019 by Amelia Joyce.

Special revised edition published to celebrate
Galway European Capital of Culture 2020.

Programme of events:

Galway European Capital of Culture 2020: www.galway2020.ie
Music *for* Galway & Galway 2020 present Sound*Scapes*: www.musicforgalway.ie
Galway International Arts Festival 2020: www.giaf.ie

ISBN: 978-1-9160393-0-8

Book design by Austin Lambe

You are invited to visit my website at
www.myconnemarajourneys.com

Dedication

To the Joyces of Joyce Country

Connemara

Acknowledgements

I wish to express my appreciation to Austin Lambe for designing this special Galway 2020 edition of *My Connemara Journeys*, Eleanor Collier for writing the foreword, Marianne ten Cate for proof reading, Andrew Pollock for his wise council and Kieran Tobin for exhibiting a collection of his landscape paintings of Connemara at the 2018 book launch in the Oughterard Courthouse.

My sincere thanks to the following Courthouse Committee members and volunteers for their support: Tom Welby, Leslie Lyons, Tom and Gil Cusack, Jess Walsh, Olga Magliocco and Ruud Wijnen.

I am grateful to family and friends for their welcome encouragement: the Joyce family; Hugh and Loretto O'Malley; Patrick and Patricia Flood; Beatrice Lawless; JP Speyart van Woerden; David O'Reilly; Garrett and Breda Byrne; Bill Daly; Sean Leonard; Patrick and Dixie O'Reilly; Patrick McGinley; Stephen, Mark, Shane and Ivan Allen; David Burke; Tomas de Brún and Mary O'Reilly-de Brún; Mary O'Dea; Benny and Grace Jennings; Tom Gibbons and family; Fr Robert McNamara; Joy and Michael Duignan; Doug and Irene Farrelly; Cora and Kate O'Brien; Julia and Bernie O'Neill; Mary Maguire; Eileen Lydon; Charlotte Barry; Ann Watts; Nicholas and Irene Lambe; Isobel Bednarek; Stephen Walsh; Gerald V. Breen, California; Hilda and Frank Furminger, California; Mary Kay Miller, La Jolla, California; Betty Hiller, La Jolla, California; Linda Dalessio and Paul Lavelle, Boston; Richard Yurko, Connecticut; Tom and Mary Barry, Michigan. A special thanks to my fellow book club members who enjoy a good read and much fun: Christine Boender, Myriam O'Reilly, Doc Gilbert, Bridget Sinnott and Catherine Conroy.

With gratitude to my mother Marty, who passed on her love of Connemara to me and to my father John for his generosity and indomitable spirit.

To the unsung heroes: well done and thanks to Paddy and Una O'Halloran, Joe and Noreen Feeney, Mary Doyle, Gerry Doyle and Ann Nash for their dedication to keeping the village of Oughterard looking so attractive during the summer season.

Foreword

For Amelia Joyce, this guidebook is a labour of love. One of Amelia's passions in life is sharing her knowledge and love of this special place and she does so beautifully in *My Connemara Journeys*, imparting her personal stories and a flavour of the history and character of Connemara, its people and the grandeur and power of its landscapes.

The great-great-grandfather of Amelia Joyce - Big Jack Joyce - came from Leenane and once owned the Leenane Inn, now known as the Leenane Hotel. The family was mostly involved in the wool trade, the main industry in this wild, craggy landscape.

Amelia enjoyed a magical childhood in this enchanting area of Connemara, climbing the rugged mountains in Leenane, swimming in Killary Harbour and picnicking on Lettergesh Beach. "The silence was everywhere, enveloping the blue sky, the icy lakes and the misty purple mountains. Apart from the bleating of the blackface sheep, the only sound to be heard was the haunting cry of the curlew and the echo of my own footsteps."

The family moved from Connemara to Dublin when Amelia was a young girl. Upon leaving boarding school she lived in Paris, before returning to Dublin a number of years later to work side-by-side with Neillí Mulcahy, one of Ireland's most famous fashion designers. Amelia followed this with a number of years making her mark in PR internationally with Intercontinental Hotels.

After her marriage to William 'Bill' Lynch in the Garden of Gethsemane, she lived in Jordan for a number of years. While in the Middle East, Amelia visited and was fascinated by the ancient cities of Petra, Syria, Aqaba and Beirut; one of her highlights was horse-riding in the vast Wadi Rum Desert, also known as the Valley of the Moon, where Lawrence of Arabia fought his battles with the Turks. A later adventure included sailing down the Amazon to Rio de Janeiro, Buenos Aires and to South Georgia Island to pay her respects to explorer Ernest Shackleton.

An evacuation from the Middle East in 1967 led to a move to La Jolla,

California, where Amelia worked in interior design. Bill received a PhD in English and American Literature from the University of California, San Diego, where he served as dean and faculty member.

Having lived abroad for over thirty years, Amelia returned to Connemara and built her dream cottage on a hill overlooking Lough Corrib; to quote Amelia:

> Living here is like being surrounded by a priceless artwork – the most beautiful living painting you can imagine, especially when the dawn breaks and the sun rises over Lough Corrib.

Eleanor Collier

Introduction

Dear Traveller,

How do you signpost Connemara, one of the most mystical places on the planet? And how on earth do you convey the magnetic, mesmerising pull of this quintessentially Celtic corner of Ireland, its ethereal beauty and the spirit and warmth of the western people?

It's not an easy task, but who better to be your guide in *'My Connemara Journeys'* than I, Amelia Joyce, a descendant of a proud and ancient clan that gave its name to the rugged splendour between Lough Corrib and Killary Harbour – Joyce Country.

My guidebook, consisting of seven journeys, provides a sprinkling of history and an insight into the lives of the extraordinary people who have lived here over the centuries. It is a pleasure for me to take you on journeys to my favourite off-the-beaten-track gems that the average tourist never sees, and to suggest places where you can enjoy afternoon tea, a creamy pint or a picnic on one of the many sandy beaches dotted along the coast.

What was once an isolated landscape ravaged by poverty has now become the destination for nature-lovers, mountain-climbers and other sports enthusiasts. Excellent restaurants are in abundance, and the choice of accommodation ranges from simple bed-and-breakfasts to world-renowned luxury castles.

The following quote captures my feelings for this wild, majestic place:

> And you feel that if God chose a place to reveal Himself it would be upon these western hills at sunset when the whole hushed world is tense with beauty and earth seems waiting for a revelation.

(In Search of Ireland by H.V. Morton)

The eighty-one years I've lived on this earth have been full of adventures but writing about Connemara has been the most rewarding, and it is my hope that in some small way these journeys will hold treasured memories for you.

Amelia Joyce

MORS AUT HONORABILIS VITA

JOYCE

Connemara

*There's something sleeping in my breast
That wakens only in the West.
There's something in the core of me
That needs the West to set it free.*

(Oliver St John Gogarty)

Oughterard

My favourite season in the west of Ireland is the springtime, when suddenly, without warning, the cuckoo announces its arrival, the mayfly rises from the bottom of the shallows, the lambs are frolicking in the fields, and the purple rhododendrons will presently set the countryside ablaze with colour. I wonder at our passion for faraway places, when the wild and exotic are so close at hand, no more so than in Oughterard, Co. Galway.

To discover this delightful area, take the N59 from Galway to Oughterard, considered the gateway to Connemara. Because of its tranquil setting on Lough Corrib, it is especially favoured by anglers, who return year after year to fish for wild salmon and brown trout.

Oughterard village is the perfect place to stop and visit before commencing your seven journeys through Connemara. Upon entering the village, there is a graveyard of note, as James Joyce selected it as the final resting place of Michael Furey in his book *The Dead*, which was hailed by Richard Ellman as a masterpiece. Apparently, Joyce was proud to bear the name of one of the tribes of Galway and his connection with Joyce Country, explaining to his London literary agent that "the family comes, of course, from the west of Ireland [Joyce Country] but mine is a southern offshoot of the tribe." Sir William Wilde, archaeologist, writer, surgeon and father of Oscar, spent his holidays at Moytura House, overlooking Lough Corrib, and in later years wrote his book *Wilde's Lough Corrib*. According to local lore, the lake boasts 365 islands, including Inchagoill, the largest and most famous. A number of monastic sites on the island date as far back as the fourth century. There is a church believed to have been built by St Patrick and his nephew Lugna, who reputedly served as the saint's navigator. Most fascinating is an obelistical pillar standing about 75cm tall with a very ancient inscription, in Roman lettering of the fifth or sixth century, understood to be the second-oldest Christian inscription in Europe. Every day at noon in July and August (except on Tuesdays), the *Corrib Queen* sails from the Pier in Oughterard to Inchagoill Island and the village of Cong on the eastern shore of Lough Corrib. The charming captain, David Luskin, is a local historian and a wonderful storyteller - a must-do tour.

Aughnanure Castle

As you approach Oughterard from Galway, you will see a large sign on your right directing you to Aughnanure Castle. This 16th century castle was one of the many strongholds of the powerful O'Flaherty clan that held sway over the west for over 400 years. It is particularly well preserved and a fine example of an Irish tower house, with the remains of a banqueting hall, watchtower, an unusual double bawn and bastions. In 1546, the legendary Grace O'Malley (Granuaile in Irish), whose exploits on the high seas earned her the title 'Pirate Queen', married Donal O'Flaherty, the head of the 'ferocious' O'Flaherty clan.

Currarevagh House

On the Glann Road, running north-east out of Oughterard, Currarevagh House sits on the banks of Lough Corrib, surrounded by acres of mature woodland with rhododendrons brought back from India by the generation of Hodgsons who originally built the house in 1842. This Victorian house possesses an informal appeal, where guests easily discover the art of gracious living. The owners, Harry, June, their son Henry and his wife Lucy, enjoy welcoming their guests, and great care is taken to ensure that they have a memorable holiday experience. June's *joie de vivre* is infectious and her creative flair is evident throughout the house, especially in the arrangements of wild flowers collected from the surrounding woodland. The food is superlative and features locally caught salmon and trout. Guests will find lots to do, including fishing, croquet, tennis, hill-walking, visiting local pubs, or the simple pleasure of sitting by the lake. Phone: 091-552312 - www.currarevagh.com.

Tourist Information Point: Check at the Camp Street Cafe for up-to-date news on the annual Oughterard Show, lectures, art exhibitions, theatre and more. www.thecampstreetcafe.com.

ATTRACTIONS

Aughnanure Castle: www.oughterardtourism.com

Oughterard Pony Show: www.oughterardshow.com

Oughterard Golf Club: https://oughterardgolfclub.com

Boat Trip to Inchagoill Island and Cong: www.corribcruises.com

Theatre in Connemara: www.curlewtheatre.com

Connemara Guided Weekend walks/Hikes:
www.connemarahikes.ie

Oughterard Walks: www.oughterardtourism.com

Glengowla Mines: www.glengowlamines.ie

Gift Shop: John P. Keogh Gifts & Crafts. Henry's shop is a treasure trove of Irish souvenirs and an abundance of other delights.

Recommended Restaurants: Halloran's, The Lake Hotel, The Boat Inn, The Greenway Café and Powers Thatch.
The White Gables in Moycullen is owned by Ann and Kevin Dunne. Kevin, the chef, has a passion for good food and his love of life is a joy. Phone: 091-555744 - www.whitegables.com

Traditional Pubs and Music: Powers Thatch, The Boat Inn and Hessions.

Sullivan's Country Grocer: This old-style country grocery store is a favourite with everyone - offering organic fruits, vegetables, freshly baked goods, and in-house cooking. A big thank you to the owner Elizabeth Folgen and her son Sianail. Phone: 091-866522 - www.sullivanscountryliving.com

Suggested Reading: *A Guide to Lough Corrib's Early Monastic Sites* by Anthony Previté.

Recommended Western Way Walk: Leaving Oughterard in the direction of Clifden, take a sharp right when you cross the bridge onto the Scenic Road to the picnic area where you can enjoy a superb view of Lough Corrib and its many islands. **Western Way** 9km Trail: Continue onto the Glann Road to the Hill of Doon. From here the **Western Way** continues through a wilderness with sweeping views of Lough Corrib, and emerges at the Maam Valley on the R336 between Maam Cross and Maum.

From Oughterard, continue on the N59 towards Connemara. Beyond Sweeney's Hotel, on your right, you will see Clareville House; built in the 18th century as a winter residence for the Martin family of Ballynahinch Castle. At a later date, the house was sold to Lucinda Elizabeth Shaw, the mother of the Irish dramatist George Bernard Shaw. Another well-known person who lived not far from Oughterard at Costello was J. Bruce Ismay, Chairman of the White Star Line, the company that owned the *Titanic*. Ismay spent many of his reclusive years in a house known as Costello Lodge.

Just 3km from Oughterard in the direction of Maam Cross, is the much photographed little stone bridge immortalised in John Ford's film, *The Quiet Man*.

Maam Cross

This historic crossroad leads to all corners of Connemara. Yes, the world has moved on, but little has changed at the Maam Cross Fair that takes place every Saturday, and especially the 'Big Fair Day' on the Tuesday after the bank holiday in October. This traditional event draws Connemara pony enthusiasts from around the world. Some believe the sturdy ponies are likely to have first appeared during the 16th century when Spanish horses, probably originating in Andalusia, came ashore from the ship-wrecked Armada and bred with the native stock. Others suggest that this is mere legend and they are descendants from the Scandinavian ponies brought to Ireland by the Vikings. Whatever their origin, their temperament, versatility and charm make them well suited to jumping and dressage.

ATTRACTIONS

Maam Cross Connemara Pony show is held in July and the Big Fair Day is in October: www.maamcrossmart.com

Peacockes Hotel: Their restaurant deserves a special mention. An excellent carvery is served daily from March to September 12:30pm - 5:00p.m. Winter months served on Sunday from 12:30pm - 6.00pm. Live music every Sunday 3.00pm - 5.00pm. The Gift Shop has something for everyone. The Burke family from Clonbur own the hotel. Phone: 091-552306 - www.peacockes.ie

---

JOURNEY 1: Clifden

Maam Cross via Recess, Lough Inagh and Letterfrack to Clifden

As you leave the sheltered tree-lined confines of Oughterard on the road to Maam Cross we are greeted by a new world, an open landscape of hills, bogs, rock and water. This is Connemara, a landscape so different that it has excited the senses of artists, writers, scientists and travellers for centuries. It is a landscape that is hostile and uncompromising yet appealing and intriguing. It is a challenge to our senses and to our intellect.
(*The Natural History of Connemara* by Tony Whilde)

From Maam Cross, continue towards Clifden on the N59. Every turn in the road opens up new, sweeping vistas of valleys, rivers, lakes, forests and mountains, adorned in a kaleidoscope of colour. May and early June are truly beautiful months in Connemara, when the entire valley is aflame with golden gorse and the purple rhododendrons are in full bloom. The village of Recess will be your first port of call.

Recess

This tranquil village was once a busy hub for visitors to Connemara. In 1895, The Great Western Railway Company opened a rail line from Galway to Clifden with the intention to improve communications with a developing fishing and tourist industry. Recess soon became a popular destination for the Irish landed gentry and English visitors to hunt, shoot and fish in the surrounding area. Luxury accommodation was provided by The Railway Hotel, and when the hotel was burned down during the Civil War in 1922, the local people suffered great hardship as the hotel had been the main source of employment in the area. A photograph of the hotel is displayed in Paddy Festy's Bar in the village. The old station house, the first two-storey house beyond the village on your left, was the location of the railway station. For Connemara people, taking this train was not for pleasure – they

were on their long journey into exile in search of a better life. Today, the village attracts tourists and writers. The legendary American Charles Kuralt, whose programme *On the Road with Charles Kuralt* was watched by millions in the USA, enjoyed visiting Connemara, where his long-time companion Patricia Shannon owned a cottage close to Recess. The English poet laureate Ted Hughes and Assia Wevill lived for a period in 1966 in nearby Cashel. Do take the time to stop and visit Joyce's Craft Shop and Art Gallery. www.joycescraftshop.com

Lough Inagh Valley

Directly across the road from the station house, take the R344 through the Inagh Valley. This deserted valley never fails to take my breath away, as here the full glories of the Connemara landscape are revealed. All around you is a lavish drama of mountains and lakes; the Maumturk Mountains dominate the right-hand side of the road, the shimmering Derryclare Lough and Lough Inagh are on the left, and the ever-present Twelve Bens frame the western horizon. The only signs of life are the blackface sheep strolling along the winding road, showing off their designer wool coats with a vibrant splash of colour.

Stop at Lough Inagh Lodge, overlooking the shores of Lough Inagh and the towering Twelve Bens. The view from this handsome 19th century fishing lodge is a David Lean epic and worthy of an Oscar. The lodge represents all that is good about Irish hospitality, with log fires, delicious food and a warm welcome from owner Máire O'Connor and her brother Dominic Moran. In the bar you will enjoy the company of Thomas Moran the barman, mountain climbers, walkers and fishermen, and you may even have the pleasure of meeting a local character by the name of Patrick Joyce. He is the tall man with the black, Spanish eyes, a tweed cap and a rich brogue that is reminiscent of times past. Phone: 095-34706 - www.loughinaghlodgehotel.ie.

Recommended Western Way hike: Park your car at the small parking lot before Lough Inagh Lodge and follow the sign across the road in the direction of Máméan, 'The Pass of the Birds'. This mystical valley is a place of wonder, solitude and reflection. St Patrick reputedly arrived here in the fourth century to bless Connemara. To this day, it is still a place of pilgrimage, with a holy well, a statue of St Patrick and the ruins of a small church nestled deep in the Maumturk Mountains between the Inagh and Maam valleys.

Over sixty years ago, I remember going to an American wake in Lough Inagh Valley for two young girls emigrating to America; there was music, dancing, a large quantity of poitín and a deep, concealed sadness beneath the joviality. There was the possibility that they would never see the girls again.

When you arrive at the end of the R344, turn left. Kylemore Lough will be on your left, opposite Kylemore House, which was built in 1785 by Lord Ardilaun, a member of the famous Guinness family. Later, it was rented by Irish author Dr Oliver St John Gogarty. It is now run as a fishing lodge.

ATTRACTIONS

Lough Inagh Lodge: Fishing, cycling, guided walking tours and art classes. Charming wedding venue. Pet-friendly.
Walks: Kevin Corcoran's book - *West of Ireland Walks* is highly recommended.

Kylemore Abbey

A few kilometres on, you will drive around a corner to be met with the Gothic extravaganza that is known as Kylemore Abbey. On a fine day, when the Abbey is reflected in the lake, you could ask yourself: "Is this a mirage? How can such a place exist?"

The extraordinary story behind Kylemore Abbey reads like a romantic novel. A brilliant young doctor named Mitchell Henry and his wife Margaret, came to Connemara on their honeymoon in 1849. They were both enchanted by the area and, as a token of his love for Margaret, Mitchell built her a breathtaking fairy-tale castle dramatically located on Lough Pollacappul. Mitchell was the son of Alexander Henry, a wealthy industrialist from the north of England with family ties to Ireland. After the death of his father in 1862 Mitchell decided to abandon his medical career to take over the family business. He was considered one of the wealthiest young men in Britain at the time.

The building of the castle brought much-needed employment to the area, which had been devastated by the Famine in the 1840s. It took four years and vast sums of money to accomplish the Henrys' dream – white granite was imported by ship from Scotland, green Connemara marble was used extensively, and Italians were brought over to plan the gardens. Heated greenhouses were built in which bananas, pineapples, oranges, nectarines and other tropical fruit was grown.

Mitchell Henry had been elected MP for Galway County from 1871-1885 and felt a great responsibility for the welfare of the people in Connemara. In a letter to the Bord of Guardian of the Glenamaddy Union he writes: "So long as I remain in Parliament, I shall pursue the same policy that I have always done, that is to endeavour to promote the practical good of the country and to speak the truth so far as I know it."

The Henrys lived happily in their new home with their nine children until tragedy struck in 1874 when Margaret died on a visit to Egypt. She was 45. Her husband built an exquisite, miniature neo-Gothic church in her memory on the grounds of the castle, one of the jewels of Irish architecture. When his daughter Geraldine was killed in 1892 in a carriage accident he was heartbroken. These tragedies on top of bad investments forced Mitchell Henry to sell his magnificent property. He returned to

England with his family in 1902, leaving behind a legacy that will live forever in the annals of Connemara history.

Henry died in 1910 and was laid to rest with his beloved wife Margaret at Kylemore. In the words of Oscar Wilde: "Behind every exquisite thing that existed, there was something tragic" (*The Picture of Dorian Gray*).

In 1903, Kylemore was purchased by the ninth Duke of Manchester. His wife, Helena Zimmerman, was an American heiress from Cincinnati, the only daughter of oil and railway tycoon Eugene Zimmerman. It was rumoured that Helena's father had contributed to the purchase of the castle and was not happy about her marriage to the duke, who was a notorious spendthrift with a reputation for high stakes gambling. When he first took over the estate he was considered a good landlord but due to excessive spending on a lavish lifestyle the property gradually fell into decline. The estate was taken over in 1914 by London Banker Ernest Fawake, until a suitable buyer was found.

The castle finally came under new ownership in 1920 when it was bought by the Irish Benedictine nuns for £45,000. The nuns had been based for generations in Belgium but forced to leave when their Abbey in Ypres was destroyed during World War I. For the next 80 years, the sisters ran an exclusive boarding school for girls, now known as Kylemore Abbey. Many moons ago, I visited the Abbey on occasions to visit my father's cousin, Sister Mary Raphael Conroy (1944-1994). My sister Margaret (Joyce) Brereton attended summer school at Kylemore, and remembers her time there with great fondness. Sadly, the school finally closed in 2010. Kylemore's ethos of education however continues. Welcome news was announced in 2015 when a 30 year partnership was agreed between Kylemore Abbey and the Catholic American University of Notre Dame, to create a new academic centre of excellence. Mitchell Henry and his wife Margaret can now continue to rest in peace while their magnificent home will remain a place of spirituality and education.

ATTRACTIONS

Tour of Kylemore Abbey. Neo-Gothic Church. Victorian Walled Garden. Mitchell's Café - www.kylemoreabbey.com

Suggested Reading: *History of Kylemore Castle & Abbey* by Kathleen Villiers-Tuthill.

Letterfrack

James and Mary Ellis, a Quaker couple from Bradford in England, moved to Letterfrack in 1849 to assist in the post-famine relief effort. There, they paid for the building of homes, a school, a doctor's dispensary and a shop. "A finer race of people no one could wish to see" wrote Mary. These good Samaritans saved a whole population from ruin. The following quote is attributed to Quaker activist Stephen Grellet: "I expect to pass through this world but once. Any good, therefore, that I can do, or any kindness I can show to any fellow creature, let me do it now. Let me not defer or neglect it, for I shall not pass this way again."

Take time to visit the visitors' centre at the Connemara National Park in Letterfrack. This impressive centre exhibits the development of the Connemara landscape over 10,000 years. One can opt for a short walk or a two-hour hike to the top of the 400 metre high Diamond Hill, the park's undisputed highlight. The rugged terrain consists of 5,000 acres including bogs, woodlands and four of the Twelve Bens.
Phone: 095-41054 - www.connemaranationalpark.ie.

Clifden

Continue on your drive towards Clifden. This vibrant, busy town was founded in 1812 by John D'Arcy (1785-1839). A man of drive, determination and foresight, D'Arcy could see the potential in this poverty-stricken area. His first achievement was to obtain government funding for the building of roads and a quay on Clifden Bay. Over time, the town developed and prospered, as cargo ships could now anchor at the quay to unload goods and export products such as marble, corn, fish, wool and kelp.

John D'Arcy built an imposing castle in a dramatic setting overlooking Clifden Bay on the Sky Road. Eventually the family were bankrupted by the Great Famine of the mid-1840s. All that remains of the castle today is a ruin silhouetted against the sky. These haunting ruins are shrouded in myth and mystery and reflect the very heart of Ireland's history.

Two major events occurred on the outskirts of Clifden. In 1907, Guglielmo Marconi exchanged the first transatlantic radio message with a station in St Johns in Newfoundland, for which he received the Nobel Prize. The other notable event was the landing in 1919 of the first transatlantic flight by Captain John Alcock and Lieutenant Arthur Whitten Brown, who were knighted for their historic achievement by King George V.

Why not bring your journey to a perfect end by picking up some gourmet items at The Connemara Hamper on Lower Market Street, and drive out the Sky Road to Eyrephort Beach for a picnic? From the beach there are views of two islands in the distance - Turbot Island and Inishturk. Some years ago, there was great excitement when an archaeological dig uncovered a grave with items that included Viking armour and a shield dating back to the ninth century. The well-known Irish actor Peter O'Toole lived in the area and considered Connemara to be his spiritual home.

ATTRACTIONS

The Connemara Smoke House: Located at Bunowen Pier in Ballyconneely - www.smokehouse.ie

The famous Connemara Pony Show in August: www.cpbs.ie

The Clifden Arts Festival in September: www.clifdenartsfestival.ie

The Station House Museum: www.connemara.net

Connemara Golf Links: www.connemaragolflinks.com

Horse Racing: On Omey Strand at Claddaghduff - www.connemara.net

Explore Connemara with Archaeologist Michael Gibbons: www.walkingireland.com

Recommended Restaurants: Marconi's, Mitchell's, Steam Café, Rosleague Manor located 15 minutes (by car) from Clifden.

Traditional Pubs and Music: Lowry's and Mullarkey's.

Fashion Shops: Millars Connemara and Hehirs of Clifden.

Book Shop: Clifden Book Bookshop.
Phone: 095-22020 - www.clifdenbookshop.com

Gift Shop: Avoca Letterfrack Café and Store. This hidden gem offers an excellent selection of exclusive gifts.

Furniture Design College: Letterfrack - www.gmit.ie

Suggested Reading: *Grace O'Malley: The Biography of Ireland's Pirate Queen 1530-1603* by Anne Chambers.

JOURNEY 2: Cong Village

Maam Cross via Maum, Finny, Clonbur, Cong, Cornamona to Maum

Such a heartbreaking symphony in blue is rarely seen in the world. There is sorrow in it, as there is in all sharp beauty. Standing there, with the gulls crying and the larks shivering in the sky and the wind going through the heather, a man goes cold with the beauty of it and is glad to be alone.
(*In Search of Ireland* by H.V. Morton)

At Peacockes Hotel at Maam Cross, turn right to Maum; here the signpost to Cong points to the right, but instead, take the R336 towards Leenane. On the way, stop off at the small Kilmilkin Church on your left to view the stained-glass window by the distinguished artist Evie Hone (1894-1955) whose most important work *The Last Supper* was created for the east window in Eton College. The Kilmilkin Church window depicts St Brendan and commemorates John Francis O'Malley, a well-known Harley Street surgeon who was born in Kilmilkin. His brother, Connor O'Malley, a professor of ophthalmology, married my aunt, Sarah 'Sal' Joyce, an anaesthetist. Conor volunteered for the British army during WW1 and was a doctor aboard a Royal Navy ship. Another brother, Tommy, was my godfather. The O'Malley tree reads like a medical encyclopedia – at last count in 1988, over forty descendants of the O'Malley clan from Kilmilkin practised medicine. Continue to Leenane and take a right to Lough Nafooey and Finny on the L1301.

Lough Nafooey

Without a doubt, Lough Nafooey forms one of the most thought-provoking scenes in Connemara. There is a deep melancholy here, but also an intense grandeur. Scattered around the never-ending hillsides are the ruins of stone cottages, abandoned in 1845 during the Great Famine. Descend the steep hill and, when the road levels, drive slowly as the entrance to the beach is narrow and easy to miss.

Sit here a while on the golden sand, listening to the sombre murmur of the waves, and be comforted in the knowledge that this compelling scene that captures the soul will always be a monument to the people who once lived here.

About five minutes from the beach, on the left side of the road, there is a sign for Joyce Country Sheepdogs. Here, Joe Joyce will be delighted to share his love of sheep farming with you and give demonstrations on how his border collies herd the mountain blackface sheep. www.joycecountrysheepdogs.ie.

Cong

Continue through the village of Clonbur to Cong. This charming village is steeped in mediaeval, cinematic history, and is the location of Ashford Castle, situated on the edge of Lough Corrib. Dating back to 1228, the castle has a history of High Kings and fabled legends, passing eventually into the hands of the Guinness family in 1882. Over the centuries, the family spent fortunes developing the property, building roads and planting thousands of trees. The last member of the Guinness family to live at the castle was Sir Arthur Edward Guinness – also known as Lord Ardilaun – with his wife, Lady Olivia Ardilaun. Devastated after her husband's death in 1915, Lady Olivia had an obelisk erected in his memory beside a romantic chalet overlooking Lough Corrib. When translated from French into English, the inscription on the obelisk reads: "Nothing remains to me any longer; anything that remains means nothing." There is an ideal picnic area close to the chalet where you can sit and enjoy scenic views of the lake.

During the years that followed, Ashford Castle was run as a hotel by various owners, and played host to many notables including King George V of England, Princess Grace and Prince Rainier III of Monaco, President Ronald Reagan, John Ford, John Wayne, Maureen O'Hara, John Lennon, Pierce Brosnan, Rory McIlroy and many others. In 2013, the castle was sold to Red Carnation Hotel Collection, headed by Bea and Stanley Tollman who said at the time that they planned to recreate a "luxurious jewel". This is exactly what they have achieved and it is now one of the leading hotels in the world. Here is a luxury hotel that breathes an atmosphere of friendly splendour. To make your visit memorable, don't miss the chance to treat yourself to their Traditional Afternoon Tea in Lady Ardilaun's drawing room. Advance booking is required. Phone: 094-9546003 - www.ashfordcastle.com.

Visit Cong Abbey, and walk in the footsteps of the Augustinian monks who lived here during the eleventh century. The original monastery that occupied this site was founded by St Feichin, a seventh century Irish saint. Cong Abbey was a place of worship and learning and a shelter for the poor and the sick. The vandalism of the monasteries under the reign of King Henry VIII resulted in an irrevocable loss of heritage that can only be described as a cultural tragedy.

Cinematic history was made in Cong in 1952 with the filming of John Ford's classic *The Quiet Man*, starring John Wayne, Maureen O'Hara and Barry Fitzgerald. For Ford, this film was a personal tribute to his ancestral homeland – his father, John Augustine, had emigrated to America from Spiddal, Co. Galway, in 1872. When the film was released it became an international success and earned Oscars for John Ford and cinematographers Winton Hoch and Archie Stout. Overnight, this remote village in the west of Ireland became the destination for tourists from around the world in search of the awe-inspiring landscapes portrayed in *The Quiet Man*.

My mother's sister, Etta Vaughan from Moycullen, was selected by John Ford to be Maureen O'Hara's stand-in. Etta – who, to the great amusement of the film crew, had never been to see a film – now found herself surrounded by the Hollywood elite. John Ford suggested she come to Hollywood and try a career in acting, while actor Ward Bond repeatedly wooed her with the words "little red-hen, can I take you back to America with me? Etta was flattered by their attention, but graciously declined. Sometime later, Etta married Bernard O'Sullivan.

Return to Maum via Cornamona. This is a magnificent drive, with expansive views of Lough Corrib and its many islands. The island you see in the distance, with the ruins of a 12th century castle, is known as Hen's Island, once occupied by the famous 'Pirate Queen' of Connemara, Grace O'Malley (1530-1603). Grace is buried in the Cistercian Abbey on Clare Island, Co. Mayo.

Maum

The well-known Scottish engineer Alexander Nimmo (1783-1832) lived at Corrib Lodge in Maum, now known as Keane's Bar. Nimmo was responsible for improving the prosperity of the Connemara region by opening up the area in 1813 to transport and communications. Jack Hanley, the charismatic barman at Keane's has worked there for over twenty years and is one of the most popular men around. Whatever the occasion, he takes care of everyone, and if you're searching for long-lost relatives in the area, he will know where to find them. A Connemara cocktail named in Jack's honour would be a fine legacy to him!

JOURNEY 3: Roundstone

Maam Cross via Ros Muc and Carna, Cashel to Roundstone

These people have learned not from books, but in the field, in the woods,
on the river bank. Their teachers have been the birds themselves,
when they sang to them, the sun when it left a glow of crimson behind
it at setting, the very trees and wild herbs.
(Anton Chekhov - 1860-1904)

When you arrive at the crossroads at Maam Cross, turn left on the R336 in the direction of Ros Muc. Here, one wonders how anyone possesses the fortitude to live in such an isolated landscape. Yet, it is this very landscape that has inspired many authors, including Pádraic Ó Conaire, Patrick Pearse, John O'Donohue and Tim Robinson, whose works have become not just part of our lives, but part of our landscapes. The highly-respected poet and philosopher John O'Donohue PhD found the inspiration here to write his book *Anam Cara*, which means 'soul friend' in the Irish language. It became an international bestseller in 1998. Over the years, I enjoyed listening to John describing the glories of Connemara on BBC World Service. Sadly, John O'Donohue died in 2008 at the age of fifty-two. www.johnodonohue.com.

Ros Muc

This winding road, set against a landscape of mountains and brown bogs, possesses a melancholy that is not so easily forgotten. As you approach Ros Muc, the impressive building you see directly facing you is Screebe Lodge. The lodge was owned in the latter half of the 19th century by Richard Berridge, a wealthy brewer from London.

Around 1902, William Humble Ward, the second Earl of Dudley, was appointed Lord Lieutenant of Ireland. Lord Dudley and his beautiful wife, Lady Rachel Dudley, often leased Screebe Lodge as a summer residence. When Lady Dudley first visited Ros Muc she was profoundly shocked

by the destitution of the local people, and immediately established a fund to provide district nurses to Connemara. Using her husband's considerable influence, she persuaded the government, her friends and Sir Ernest Shackleton to contribute to the foundation. Thanks to her commitment, The Lady Dudley Nurses eventually provided care to the neglected counties throughout the western seaboard. This remarkable woman was awarded the CBE and the Royal Red Cross for her outstanding services to humanity. Lady Dudley died in 1920 from a heart attack while swimming in Camus Bay, Ros muc. Over the years, Screebe Lodge has had many owners. Today it is owned by the Burkart family and is run as a luxury hotel known as Screebe House. Phone: 091-574110 - www.screebe.com.

Patrick Pearse's Cottage

Continue on the R340 towards Carna. You are now entering the Gaeltacht, where Gaelic is the primary spoken language. This is where Patrick Pearse (1879-1916), the impassioned idealist, dedicated himself to Irish nationalism and the Gaelic language, and in 1909 built himself a retreat, a thatched cottage perched on a knoll overlooking Loch Oiriúlach. Here, in the heart of the Gaeltacht, was a perfect place to illuminate his dream of a free and Gaelic Ireland.

In this tranquil setting, Pearse's cottage became one of the secret meeting places for members of the Irish Republican Brotherhood to plan the insurrection against the British. The young leader of the 1916 Easter Rising was a most unlikely military leader, a shy man, a poet, whose main interests were education, law and literature.

On Easter Monday, 24 April 1916, Patrick Pearse read The Proclamation of the Irish Republic to the people of Ireland outside the General Post Office in Dublin, signalling the start of the Easter Rising. Their forces had no chance of victory against the might of the British army, and surrendered six days later. They were later charged with treason and executed by firing squad in Kilmainham Gaol. Fourteen of the leaders including Patrick Pearse are buried in Amber Hill Cemetery, located near The National Museum-Collins Barracks in Dublin. Kilmainham Gaol is now a museum, visited by hundreds of thousands of people each year to pay homage to the freedom fighters. The following poem was written by Patrick on the eve of his execution.

The Wayfarer

The beauty of the world hath made me sad,
This beauty that will pass;
Sometimes my heart hath shaken with great joy
To see a leaping squirrel in a tree,
Or a red lady-bird upon a stalk,
Or little rabbits in a field at evening,
Lit by a slanting sun,
Or some green hill where shadows drifted by
Some quiet hill where mountainy man hath sown
And soon would reap; near the gate of Heaven;
Or children with bare feet upon the sands
Of some ebbed sea, or playing on the streets
Of little towns in Connacht,
Things young and happy.
And then my heart hath told me:
These will pass,
Will pass and change, will die and be no more,
Things bright and green, things young and happy;
And I have gone upon my way
Sorrowful.

Major General Charles Blackader, the British officer who chaired Pearse's court martial, is reported to have said after the trial: "I have just done one of the hardest tasks I have ever had to do. I have had to condemn to death one of the finest characters I have ever come across. There must be something very wrong in the state of things that makes a man like that a rebel. I don't wonder his pupils adored him". No doubt, the major carried the memory of Patrick with him for the rest of his life.

ATTRACTIONS

A Connemara Cultural Centre: Located close to Patrick Pearse's Cottage. The centre provides an introduction to the Irish language, Gaeltacht culture and Pearse's connection to Ros Muc.
Phone: 091-574292 - www.icpconamara.ie
Café: Serves freshly baked goods.
Suggested Reading: *Easter Widows* by Sinéad McCoole.

Carna

I had the pleasure of meeting Martin 'Marty' J. Walsh, the Mayor of Boston, and Máirtín Ó Catháin, the Chairman of the Organising Committee at the opening of the New Emigrant Commemorative Centre on the 12 May 2018. The centre is a monument honouring the people who emigrated from Connemara, and exhibits dramatic and inspiring stories about their lives. Here, you can immerse yourself in the cultural traditions of our rural ancestors and research your family genealogy. Additionally, at various times throughout the year there are events for families and children, traditional music, art exhibitions and lectures - http://www.carnaemigrantscentre.com. Marty's parents, John Walsh and Mary O'Malley, had both emigrated from the Ros Muc and Carna area to America in the 1950s. When President Kennedy visited the west of Ireland in 1963 he said: "If the day was clear enough, and if you went down to the bay and you looked west, and your sight was good enough, you would see Boston, Massachusetts." The Irish have been involved in American politics as far back as 1776, when the Declaration of Independence was signed, among others, by Irishmen George Taylor, Matthew Thornton and James Smith.

Martin 'Marty' J. Walsh, Mayor of Boston

Cashel

Return towards Pearse's cottage and take a left to Cashel on the L1205. I always advise my guests to take this magnificent drive, with vistas of the Twelve Bens in the distance, and I will be very surprised if you meet a fellow traveller on this road. Take a right at the end of the road onto R340, and then a left onto the R342 towards Cashel.

Great gardens are a hallmark of western Ireland, and Cashel House has a garden to rival most. This gracious house was built in the 1840s and is owned by the McEvilly family. The fine furniture, antiques, and paintings add an old world charm and personality to every room. The elegant dining room is located in the conservatory and serves country house cooking at its best. Enjoy genuine Irish hospitality in this pleasant tranquil setting, with a panorama of rhododendrons, rare magnolias, azaleas and other exotic plants.

When General de Gaulle visited Ireland with his wife Yvonne in 1969, he chose Cashel House as his retreat to commence writing his memoir and to trace his Irish ancestors, the MacCartans, on his mother's side. When de Gaulle left, he wrote with the economy of a military man just one word in the visitors' book: "Excellent". Phone: 095-31001 - www.cashelhouse.ie.

ATTRACTIONS

Gardening and painting classes, fishing, horse-riding and walking tours. A perfect wedding venue. Open for Christmas.

Roundstone

Upon leaving Cashel House for Roundstone, you will enjoy some lovely views of Cashel Bay. When you arrive at the crossroads, turn left to Roundstone. This charming fishing village overlooking Bertraghboy Bay was designed by the Scottish engineer Alexander Nimmo in 1820. The highlight of the year is the popular Roundstone Regatta, held every July since the 1890s. Witness currachs and Galway hookers in all their glory during two days of racing.

ATTRACTIONS

Irish Music, Song and Dance: Every Wednesday in July and August at the Roundstone Community Centre at 8.30pm.

Connemara Champion Golf Links at Ballyconnelly:
www.connemaragolflinks.com

Beaches: Gurteen Bay and Dog's Bay.

Surfing: www.realadventures.ie

Recommended Restaurants: Vaughan's Restaurant at the Roundstone House Hotel. Beola Restaurant.

Traditional Pub Music: The Shamrock Bar.

Suggested Reading: *Connemara* by Tim Robinson

JOURNEY 4: Renvyle
Leenane via Rosroe, Tully Cross to Renvyle

*In Connemara, God's colour palette is alive with joyous colours. The gentle
greys blend with cornelian and indigo to cool distant blues, surprised by sudden
splashes of purple heather, moss green grasses, yellow birds-foot-trefoil and
russet gorse. Overhead the cheeky clouds send multi shaped shadows over the
scene drawing the eye to the hidden features of each mountain face. Surely,
herein this glorious part of the world Thine is the Kingdom.*
(Doc Gilbert, Oughterard, Co. Galway)

The Little Killary, Rosroe

On the way to Rosroe from Leenane on the R336 you will pass the
Leenane Hotel, renowned for its setting on Killary Harbour. The
hotel dates as far back as 1796, and was once owned (when a
simple inn) by the infamous Big Jack Joyce, who was well known for his
hospitality. It must have been quite a spectacle when, in 1899, a flotilla
of battleships, led by HMS Pelorus, anchored in Killary Harbour to shelter
from a storm. Another extraordinary sight to be witnessed by the locals
was the British fleet sailing into Killary Harbour in 1903 with King Edward
VII, Queen Alexandra and Princess Victoria aboard; they briefly visited
the Leenane Hotel before travelling onto Kylemore Castle (now known
as Kylemore Abbey) for afternoon tea. The purpose of their visit was to
inspect the local cottage industries. Over the centuries, the Leenane Hotel
has undergone extensive renovations, and today it is owned by Conor
Foyle, a member of the well-known hotelier family. During your stay at
this leisurely retreat, experience the seaweed baths – and especially
the romantic moonlight dinner cruise on Killary Harbour aboard the
Connemara Lady. Phone: 095-42249 - www.leenanehotel.com.

Seven kilometres from Leenane, take a right to Tully Cross. The first lake
on the left is Lough Fee, and the house you see peeking through the trees
was once the summer home of Oscar Wilde, Irish wit, poet and dramatist.
Oscar was very proud of his full name - Oscar Fingal O'Flahertie Wills
Wilde - connecting him to two formidable Connemara clans, namely the
feisty O'Flahertys and the Fingals. Oscar's parents, Sir William and Lady
Jane Wilde, built Illaunroe Lodge on Lough Fee in 1853. Every summer,

Oscar and his brother Willie spent their holidays here, hunting, fishing and entertaining friends. Later, Victorian England was captivated by his words and outraged by his personal life. While in prison, Oscar must have found solace in his treasured memories of Illaunroe. He died in 1900 and is buried in Père Lachaise Cemetery in Paris. In his biography of Oscar Wilde, Richard Ellman writes: "He is not one of those writers who as the centuries change lose their relevance. Wilde is one of us. His wit is an agent of renewal, as pertinent now as a hundred years ago."

The next lake on your left is Lough Muck; take the road opposite towards Little Killary at Rosroe. Along the way, the lingering ghosts who occupy the abandoned famine cottages communicate their sorrow to the passing stranger. The old hostel located at the pier was rented over the years by a number of well-known artists and writers. Paul Henry described his time here as capturing "the very soul of Ireland" in his paintings. Ludwig Wittgenstein, the renowned Austrian-British philosopher, retreated to the solitude of Rosroe to write, and former President of Ireland Mary Robinson unveiled a plaque commemorating his visit in 1993. Richard Murphy, Ireland's distinguished poet, found inspiration in this windswept isolation, writing: "I suffered the bitter harshness of stormy weather as a penance to achieve the salvation of poetry." His memoir, *The Kick*, is a page-turner. Michael Viney, writer for the *Irish Times*, described the poet: "Murphy emerged lean and hawkishly handsome, with a lasting patrician charm."

Recommended 6km Western Way hike: The hike starts close to Rosroe Pier and runs along the Famine road on the very edge of Killary Harbour. On the way you will pass through the deserted 'famine village' of Foher and emerge on the main N59 road near Leenane. The views are superb, with Mweelrea Mountain basking in the reflection of her benign image on the waters of Killary Harbour.

Return to the main road and continue towards Tully Cross along the wild Atlantic coast, passing Glassillaun Beach, which is very popular for snorkelling, surfing and scuba-diving. Further on is the long sandy beach of Lettergesh, where I spent many happy days with my mother and siblings, swimming, picnicking and crunching on sandy egg-sandwiches in the sheltered dunes. The horse-racing scene in The *Quiet Man* was filmed here.

Tully Cross

At the village of Tully Cross, visit the Catholic church to view the stained-glass windows by Harry Clarke (1889-1931), a leading figure in the Irish arts and crafts movement. The windows were donated to the church by Oliver St John Gogarty.

Renvyle House

For centuries, Renvyle belonged to the Blakes, an old Galway family who owned vast territories in Connemara dating back to the 1680s; they continued to live there until the 20th century. As landlords the Blakes were a mixed lot - some good, some bad - and like most landed families they were greatly impoverished during the 1840s. During the 1880s, Edgar and Caroline Blake turned Renvyle into a country house hotel which prospered for a while but eventually had to be sold.

In 1917, the property was sold to Oliver St John Gogarty, surgeon, novelist, poet, pilot and politician. Gogarty was a charismatic character who enjoyed a flamboyant lifestyle, and could be seen driving around

Connemara in his buttercup-yellow Rolls-Royce. At Renvyle House he created a rendezvous for the literati and intelligentsia, entertaining W.B. Yeats, Lady Gregory, Lady Lavery, John McCormick, August John, Prince Ranji and many more.

Following the ratification of the Anglo-Irish Treaty, Gogarty sided with the pro-Treaty government and was made a Free State Senator. Tragedy struck in 1923 when his cherished house was burned to the ground by anti-Treaty forces. When it was rebuilt, he and his wife Martha ran it as a hotel. Over time, Gogarty became increasingly disillusioned with Irish politics and went to the USA in 1939 for an extended lecture tour. He became an American citizen, and eventually decided to reside permanently in the USA, supporting himself by writing and lecturing. He died in New York in 1957, and is buried with his wife Martha in Cartron Church Cemetery in Moyard, near Renvyle. His gravestone is engraved with a verse of his own:

Our friends go with us as we go

Down the long path where Beauty wends,

Where all we love forgathers, so

Why should we fear to join our friends?

(1923, *Non Dolet*)

In 1952, when Renvyle House Hotel came on the market, my father was outbid by John Coyle and two other investors, who purchased the property for the reported sum of £3,000. Some time later, the Coyle family became full owners of the property. Today, Renvyle House Hotel is immensely popular, renowned for its food, hospitality and entertainment. The star of the hotel is Chief Executive Ronnie Counihan, who is greatly appreciated for his significant contribution to the success of this iconic hotel 'within a stone's throw' of the Wild Atlantic. A great location to enjoy a drink and discuss your day in 'The Land of Lakes and Legends'. Phone: 095-46100 - www.renvyle.com.

ACTIVITIES

Golf, fishing, tennis, swimming, clay-pigeon shooting. Open for Christmas. A popular venue for weddings. Pets welcome. Diamond's Equestrian Centre: www.theconnemarapony.ie

Suggested reading: *Yeats: The Man and The Masks* by Richard Ellman

---

JOURNEY 5: Ballynahinch Castle
Maam Cross via Recess to Ballynahinch Castle

*I have been to the Tomb of Tutankhamun in Egypt, but entering
Connemara gave me a finer feeling of discovery and a greater
sense of remoteness from the modern world.
(In Search of Ireland, by H.V. Morton)*

Five kilometres beyond Recess, on the N59 to Clifden, there is a sign on the left side of the road directing you to Ballynahinch Castle Hotel on the R341. The fairy-tale white gate lodge strikes a graceful pose, giving a hint of elegance and sophistication. The long, manicured driveway is surrounded by trout streams, gardens and woods harbouring a variety of wildlife. Ballynahinch has a captivating history and offers a glimpse into Ireland's past and present-day luxury. Over the years, many people, from tourists to celebrities and heads of state, have visited this unique property.

The castle stands on 700 acres under the imposing presence of Benlettery Mountain, and has been intertwined with the history of Connemara for centuries. Volumes have been written about the various owners, starting with 'the ferocious O'Flahertys' who ruled Connemara from their coastal and island castles from the 13th to the 16th century. Grace O'Malley, also known as Granuaile, the 'Pirate Queen', married Donal O'Flaherty, a union that brought together two leading families in the west. The picturesque ruin of their 16th-century castle can still be seen today on Ballynahinch Lake. Their exploits during their rule are legendary, but eventually the fate of the O'Flahertys could not be protected against the expansionary and colonial policies of the English Crown. Now, only the wandering spirits from their turbulent past protect these castles that once represented mighty symbols of power.

With the decline of the O'Flaherty reign in Connemara, another extraordinary family was waiting in the wings to take over Ballynahinch. Around 1677 Richard Martin owned the vast estate of over 200,000

acres, much of which was acquired by dubious means from the last of the O'Flahertys. Richard was a wealthy Catholic merchant and one of the fourteen tribes of Galway. This founder of the Martin family dynasty was a shrewd lawyer and a noted swordsman known as 'Nimble Dick'. During the following years the Ballynahinch household included a rich tapestry of characters including the historical figure Richard Martin MP who succeeded to the 'kingship' of Connemara when his father Robert died in 1794. He was the first in the family to be educated at Harrow and Cambridge, but retained his family's Catholic sympathies. Richard led a remarkable life that included many travelling adventures with his cousin James Jordan. One journey was a trip to America where, by chance, he happened to be in New England at the start of the American War of Independence, and another while he was living in Paris, where he witnessed the outbreak of the French Revolution. He was a skilled lawyer, a man of great charm, wit and compassion and known for his extravagant lifestyle. He was well known for his duelling skills with countless combats under his belt which earned him the name 'Hair trigger Dick'.

Richard became a Member for Galway in the Irish Parliament after the Act of Union in 1800 at Westminster, where he championed Catholic Emancipation which was eventually granted in 1829. All his life, he castigated social injustice to man or beast, and he had an aversion to capital punishment. A cause dear to his heart was campaigning for animal rights. Through his tireless work as MP the Cruel Treatment of Cattle Act, known as the 'Martin Act', was passed in 1822 by the British House of Commons. He was the chief founder of the Society for the Prevention of Cruelty to Animals – known worldwide as the RSPCA. His friend, King George VI, honoured him with the nickname 'Humanity Dick'.

Richard lost the 1826 Galway election due to his supporters voting three and four times in his favour. Losing the election was a great political blow to Richard, and more significantly, it meant he would no longer be given immunity from prosecution for his debts. To avoid going to gaol he fled with his family to Boulogne on the Normandy coast, and never again returned to his beloved Connemara. In her biography of *Humanity Dick Martin 'King of Connemara'* 1754-1834 Shevawn Lynam writes:

A year after his death, Martin's Act was extended to embrace all cruelty to all domestic animals, and the work which had absorbed so much of his heart and mind was completed. It was a contemporary on the bench, describing him at the height of his fame, who wrote the most fitting epitaph: "In life he never was equalled, and when he dies by whom shall he be replaced?"

Richard's son, Thomas Barnwell Martin (1786-1847), inherited debts of almost £100,000. He was described as a cordial, kind man who also loved to entertain and frequently invited total strangers to stop by for a chat. He adored his only daughter Mary, a clever young woman who spoke many languages and was the author of several books. Thomas was very protective of his tenants, as his father had been, but nothing could prepare him for the deathblow that was about to be dealt to Connemara. When the Great Famine of 1845 clamped its ghastly hold on Connemara, Thomas did what he could to alleviate his tenants' suffering, but tragically, he died of fever, caught while visiting them in the Clifden workhouse. He died uttering the words, "What will become of my people now!" His tenants either emigrated to America or died in agony from hunger or typhus and with no rents coming in, the estate became bankrupt.

As the sole heiress to the Martin estate, Mary had acquired the title 'Princess of Connemara'. Now having lost the family fortune, Mary and her husband, Arthur Gonne Bell, moved to Belgium where Mary turned to writing for financial support; from there they moved to New York. Not long after their arrival, Mary died in childbirth in 1850. In the same year, her husband published her romantic novel *Julia Howard,* a thoughtful portrayal of Irish peasantry, clearly influenced by her grandfather, Richard Martin.

Thomas Colville Scott was sent from London to Connemara in 1853 by Law Life Assurance Society to write a report on the Martin estate and the surrounding area. He wrote the following description of the devastation he witnessed: *Ireland Journal of a Visit to Connemara Galway*:

Humanity Dick. Colonel Richard Martin, MP

His Highness Kumar Shri Ranjitsinhji, Jam Sahib of Nawanagar

There is no Irish animation here, but a stealthy and timid look, as if the poor souls were ashamed of their condition, and lost to the faintest hope of escape from wretchedness and misery. Good God! Where are their landlords and the responsible power that rules over them: have they never looked into these all but vacant faces only animated with a faint imploring look - have they never seen the bent back of the aged, and the sunk cheek of the young? Then let them come here and see what neglect has done.

In 1872 the Law Life Assurance Society sold the Martin estate to Richard Berridge, a wealthy London brewer. It was estimated at the time that Richard Berridge was the largest landowner in Ireland. He restored and transformed the castle to its present-day structure. The family also owned Lough Inagh Lodge, Screebe Lodge and Fermoy Lodge.

Nothing prepared Connemara for the next owner of Ballynahinch Castle, an exotic Indian prince named His Highness Kumar Shri Ranjitsinhji, Jam Sahib of Nawanagar, the ruler of a small state in north-western India. 'Ranji', as he was known to his friends, played first-class cricket for Cambridge University and was regarded as a superstar, the greatest batsman of all time. His other great passion was fly-fishing. When Ranji heard Ballynahinch Castle and its famous fisheries were for rent, he decided to visit Connemara in July 1924. Just like the previous owners, he fell under the spell of Ballynahinch and purchased the castle in 1925 for a reported £30,000. He renovated the castle, landscaped the gardens, planted over 30,000 trees and erected piers and fishing huts along the Owenmore River that meanders through the estate. Soon nicknamed 'the Maharajah of Connemara' by the locals, Ranji loved his life at Ballynahinch. It was his refuge, where he could spend his time fishing, relaxing with his friends and enjoying the timeless beauty of his surroundings. His residency at the castle was legendary because of his deep affection for the people on the estate. Every summer, he arrived by train, accompanied by his entourage and a selection of cars, which he gave away as gifts to the locals on his departure. Eventually he would run into debt, but he never allowed his debts to interfere with his opulent lifestyle or enjoyment of living.

The Maharajah of Connemara died in India in 1933. His ashes were taken to where the Ganges and Juma rivers meet, which is considered one of India's most sacred places. Ranji's employees at the castle, who shared neither his culture nor his religion, would always remember him as a member of their own family.

The next owners of Ballynahinch Castle included Frederick C. McCormack, the Irish Tourist Board and US businessman, Raymond Mason and his wife Minerva. Under their direction the castle underwent extensive renovation and was turned into a hotel that became a beacon of Irish hospitality.

The successful Irish businessman Denis O'Brien purchased Ballynahinch Castle Hotel in January 2014 and immediately embarked on a quest to further enhance the property. Mr O'Brien is to be congratulated for giving the old lady a major facelift without sacrificing the character and charm of the 'Grande Dame of Connemara'. The following quote from *Andrea del Sarto* by Robert Browning comes to mind: "Ah, but man's reach should exceed his grasp, Or what's a heaven for?"

When you walk through the front door at Ballynahinch Castle Hotel, you are made welcome, winter or summer, by the warm glow of a crackling fire. The essence of this hotel is its relaxed atmosphere and total lack of pretension. You will not be able to resist its charming appeal, returning again and again to enjoy its hospitality, delicious food and the incomparable splendour of Connemara. The credit for its success is due to the friendly staff, General Manager Eoin Walsh and Deputy General Manager Nick van Duijn, ambassadors extraordinaire. Before your departure from the hotel, view the portrait of Richard Martin in the study. Perhaps this is an opportune time to drink a toast to Richard, and all the other extraordinary people who have lived at Ballynahinch Castle. Phone: 095-31006 - www.ballynahinch-castle.com.

ATTRACTIONS
The very best of fly fishing in Ireland. Woodcock and clay shooting, walking/hiking. Walled garden. A romantic wedding venue.
Suggested Reading: *Humanity Dick Martin 'King of Connemara' 1754-1834* by Shevawn Lynam

---

JOURNEY 6:

Maam Cross via Glenlosh Valley to Leenane

*It has been said that there are certain places on this lovely old planet of ours,
battered and abused as she is, where people, for some mysterious reason, find
their souls, fall in love and never want to leave. And discovering Connemara
on the very edge of the Continent, bravely facing the great Atlantic,
is one of those places; where land, sky and sea seem to come together
in a dance of poetic perfection, a tribute to the Divine.*
(Gerald V. Breen - Sausalito, California)

Joyce Country

At Peacockes Hotel at Maam Cross, turn right on the R336 to Maum. From here the journey enters the Maam Valley, on the southern edge of Joyce Country, described by Oscar Wilde as "a savage beauty". This wild, untamed valley never fails to welcome me home, with its ancient canvas of towering mountains, sparkling lakes and the carefree clouds overhead, caressing the savage beauty with their passing shadows.

The area is named Joyce Country because of the vast territories the clan once owned in Connemara. According to James Hardiman, the historian of Galway, the Joyces were of Welsh and English origins; the first to arrive was a Thomas Joyce during the reign of King Edward I in the 12th century. The Joyces were renowned for their strength and exceptional height, and their family motto was 'Death Before Dishonour'. In every family there are a few characters more notable than others, and in our family there were two. My great-great-grandfather, John 'Jack' Joyce, also known as Big Jack Joyce, was described by Henry D. Inglis, in *A Journey Throughout Ireland in 1834*: "Big Jack Joyce looks upon himself as the greatest man for many a mile around: as a sort of king of that country, Joyce Country, as indeed he is. "I also found a really amusing story relating to Big Jack in *The Scenery and Antiquities of Ireland* (1842) by Joseph Sterling Coyne and William Henry Bartlett: "Since there was no Justice of the Peace in the west, Big Jack Joyce took it upon himself to settle differences amongst the neighbours by taking

the parties at variance by the nape of the neck, and battering their heads together until they consented to shake hands and drink a glass of poitín together, which of course, it was Jack's office to furnish for a consideration." Another traveller, Caesar Otway, in his book titled *A Tour of Connaught (1839)*, described Jack as he saw him in his prime: "I think a finer specimen of a strong man, tall and yet well-proportioned, I could not conceive. Milo of Crotona might have shaken hands with him as a brother, and the gifted sculptor of the Farnese Hercules might have selected Jack as his lay figure." The other character was Big Ned Joyce who is described by Patricia Kilroy in *The Story of Connemara*: "Big Ned Joyce, leading man of the predominant local family, was famous for going from ship to ship organising a fair price for [fish] for the whole community, retaining the old mantle of chief of his people."

Gleann Fhada

Take time to visit Gleann Fhada (The Long Glen). Towards the end of the road, before Maum Bridge, there is a **Western Way** signpost in the direction of Cur. Walk or drive down the Cur road, and take a left at the Y to Gleann Fhada. For me, this valley represents a natural shrine that symbolises the spirit of the land and celebrates the marvels of nature in every shade and colour.

Highly recommended is the 5km **Western Way** hike: From Gleann Fhada follow the Máméan mountain pass that takes you through a rugged Maumturk Mountain valley to the small church dedicated to St Patrick and subsequently, to the magnificent Lough Inagh valley.

Glenlosh Valley

The Blackface mountain sheep are believed to have descended from the wild, horned Argali sheep that inhabited Central Asia in ancient times. Gradually they spread west through Europe and are thought to have been introduced to mainland Britain by the Danes circa 800AD. In Connemara, the sheep were imported by the thousands from Scotland through Killary Harbour during the 1850s by an English Landlord named Captain Houstin, who owned approximately 40,000 acres stretching from Killary Harbour to Clew Bay. Over the centuries my ancestors were involved in sheep farming in Glenlosh Valley. In the 1900s, Festy Keane was the last chief herdsman to work for my father, John Martin Joyce, who was a wool merchant. Festy was a 'Diamond in the Rough' who lived an isolated life with his sheepdogs and usually only communicated with fellow farmers at Sunday Mass or on a fair day. Festy died in 1980 and is buried in Breenane Cemetery with fellow eudaemon spirits of good, bestowing protection over the valley they knew and loved. Today, many well-known sheep farmers carry on the tradition of their forefathers, chief among them Arthur Joyce of Mounterowen, Michael and Joseph O'Neill of Glencroft, Sean and Eamon Bodkin of Lough Inagh, Vin Joyce of Ashmount, Richard King of Leenane and many others, each with their own extraordinary story. My uncle, Thomas 'Francis' Joyce of Mounterowen was well-known for his community work in Leenane. My father was appointed Peace Commissioner from April 1931 - 1941.

Glenlosh Valley is also rich in prehistoric and early historic sites; Bronze Age cooking sites were revealed during the recent planting of a pine forest.

Return to the R336 and continue to Leenane. The road runs parallel with the Joyce River. Before arriving at Leenane village you will drive through Mounterowen. High on the hillside, on the left side of the road,

is Joyce Grove, the birthplace of my father. His parents, Thomas Francis Joyce and Sabina (Conroy) Joyce (from Garafin House, Ros Muc) had ten children. The eldest son Patrick died at age 29 during the 1918-1919 flu pandemic. One of their daughters was the well-known Connemara poet Dell (Joyce) Allen. In 1909, the family moved to Bay View House, overlooking Killary Harbour in Leenane. My father was called home from Blackrock College in 1922 to take over the sheep farms he had inherited from his father: a large farm in Glenlosh Valley and Garde Mountain situated on the shores of Killary Harbour.

My father later married my mother, Margaret 'Marty' Vaughan from Moycullen, and they had six children: Patricia, Sean, Mary, Ann, Margaret and myself. The family lived at Bay View House before eventually moving to Dublin, although returning to Connemara every year for the summer holidays.

Leenane

This sleepy village on Killary Harbour is surrounded by an amphitheatre of mountains, resembling temples from an ancient world. It is hard not to be overwhelmed by their majesty and the feeling that our ancestors enjoyed the same view a thousand years earlier. Our summer holidays in Leenane were magical; we loved our freedom and spent most of our time rambling the mountains like wild mountain goats discovering new pastures.

I carry with me a treasure chest of recollections from those bygone days. One of my favourites was going out fishing on the Killary with local fishermen at sunrise when the water, the clouds and the mountains were tinged gold and violet from the rising sun. The only sound to be heard was the gentle lapping of the oars and the echo of the fishermen's voices as they hauled in their nets weighed down with silver salmon. When it came time to eat we pulled the boats up onto Colonel Thompson's strand, where a salmon was cooked and served with a splash of seawater.

Eventually, Bay View House was sold to the Order of the Sisters of Mercy, and then purchased by Sean and Mary Hamilton who turned it into a successful guesthouse - www.theconvent.ie. Sean's father,

Eddie Hamilton, who had managed the business in Leenane, went on to be a successful businessman in the area. The sheep farm in Glenlosh Valley was sold to Henner Meis. My father decided to move to Dublin to expand his wool trade, and invested in lowland farms in Co. Meath. He turned his business into a successful enterprise, buying and selling wool in Europe, America and South America. He was elected President of the Irish Wool Federation in 1954. The following are two of his favourite quotes: "See yourself as a world citizen, and never confine yourself to boundaries" and "A man cannot discover new oceans unless he has the courage to lose sight of the shore". He was a man of integrity and well-known for his generosity of spirit. After his retirement he went to live in Costa Rica. Even in old age, he refused to resign and face life passively; instead, like Ulysses, he continued with his travels around the world.

> *I cannot rest from travel: I will drink*
> *Life to the lees: all times I have enjoyed*
> *Greatly, have suffered greatly, both with those*
> *That love me, and alone, on shore.*
> (Alfred Lord Tennyson)

My father died in 1992 and my dear mother Marty, whose passions in life included fine books, music, antiques, games of poker and a love of Connemara, died in 1991.

Leenane was awakened from its long slumber in 1989 when a film crew arrived to film an adaptation of John B. Keane's play *The Field*, directed by Jim Sheridan and starring Richard Harris.

ATTRACTIONS

The Sheep and Wool Centre, Gift Shop and Café.
Phone: 095-42323 - www.sheepandwoolcentre.com
The Forge is a popular gift shop overlooking Killary Harbour.
Recommended Restaurant: Local man Shane Hamilton is the owner of the Blackberry. This is a popular place for a light lunch or a full evening meal. Enjoy a selection of sea food and fresh fish caught daily in the nearby lakes and rivers. Closed on Tuesdays in May, June and September. Phone: 095-42240 - www.blackberryrestaurant.ie
Traditional Pubs & Music: Gaynor's Bar and Hamilton's Bar.
Suggested Reading: *Connemara - Visions of Iar Chonnacht* by Michael Gibbons.

JOURNEY 7:

Leenane via Aasleagh Falls to Delphi

And you feel that if God chose a place to reveal Himself it would be upon these western hills at sunset when the whole hushed world is tense with beauty and earth seems waiting for a revelation.
(*In Search of Ireland* by H.V. Morton)

Leaving Leenane, take the N59 towards Westport. St Michael's Church is situated on the hill opposite the cemetery where my parents, John and Margaret Joyce, my aunt Dell (Joyce) Allen, and my brother Sean, who had an abiding love of Connemara, are laid to rest. This sacred place blends in harmoniously with the surrounding landscape, and the occupants enjoy a 'grandstand view' of Killary Harbour that they so richly deserve.

Aasleagh Lodge

Take the next left on the R335 towards Louisburgh. As you make the turn, there is an entrance to Aasleagh Lodge on the right. This beautifully-restored Victorian house was once part of the large estate of the Marquis of Sligo, and later belonged to Lord John Brabourne and Lady Patricia Brabourne, the daughter of Earl Mountbatten. Lord Brabourne was a well-known film producer; among his most acclaimed works is *Passage to India*. While out on a family fishing trip in 1979, Lord Mountbatten, Lady Brabourne's son Nicholas, Lord Brabourne's mother, Baroness Doreen Brabourne, and a young boatman, Paul Maxwell, were tragically murdered by the IRA. The family later sold the lodge to the Irish State. The nearby Aasleagh Falls is a premier location for fishing wild Atlantic salmon on the Erriff River. www.fisheriesireland.ie.

Delphi

No tour of Connemara is complete without a visit to the stunning Delphi Valley, the 'Emerald in the Crown' of the west. As you drive on the road to Delphi you are escorted by Killary Harbour on your left. When you pass the small hamlet of Bundorragha you are now entering Delphi Valley.

The first building on your left is the Delphi Resort, which offers accommodation and a large choice of outdoor and water activities for all ages. There is an on-site restaurant and a health spa with seaweed baths, highly recommended to sooth and relax an aching body after a day of mountain climbing. www.delphiadventureresort.com.

The lakes and the Bundorragha River in Delphi Valley are famous for salmon and sea trout fishing. The first lake on the left is the location of Delphi Lodge, sitting under the majestic Sheeffry Hills with an enchanting view of Fin Lough. The Marquis of Sligo (formerly of Westport House, Co. Mayo) built Delphi Lodge in the 1830s; it is surrounded by a thousand acres of mountain, bog and water. After returning from a grand tour of Greece with Lord Byron, the Marquis named his house Delphi. In ancient times, Delphi in Greece was considered the centre of the known world and the place on earth where man was closest to God. This 'Garden of Eden' is now run as a country house hotel, attracting guests from around the world who can't resist its spellbinding scenery. General Manager Michael Wade makes everyone feel at home with his gracious, easy-going manner. A number of well-known personalities have stayed here over the years, including Prince Charles of Britain, who came here to paint; how he must have enjoyed his solitude away from the maddening crowd. Phone 095-42222 - www.delphilodge.ie.

ATTRACTIONS

A salmon anglers paradise. The Delphi Flyfishing School. Woodcock shooting. An unforgettable location for weddings.
Cottages: There are five cosy cottages for rent on the estate.
Suggested Reading: *The Great Hunger* by Cecil Woodham-Smith.

Continue on your drive by Doo Lough, set in an arena of captivating mountains, each one seeking your admiration. Sadly, the haunting beauty of the valley is marred by the reality of what took place here during the Famine when people died from starvation, humiliation and desecration of the human spirit. The memory of that time has not vanished; when darkness falls, their faint voices can still be heard in the wind as it sweeps down from the mountains through Delphi Valley.

FIVE STAR

LUXURY FIVE STAR ACCOMMODATION

WELCOME

TO

JOYCE COUNTRY, CONNEMARA

A PLACE THAT HAS INSPIRED AND CAPTURED
THE IMAGINATION OF GREAT WRITERS, ARTISTS,
MOVIE MAKERS AND POETS WHO FELL UNDER
ITS MAGICAL SPELL.

WWW.FIVESTAR.IE

Music for Galway

- an International Concert
Season for the West of Ireland

Music for Galway (MfG) offers a diverse and stimulating seasonal programme, from solo recitals to chamber music performances, operatic productions and orchestral concerts. MfG presents internationally renowned artists and regularly collaborates with the RTÉ Orchestras, the Irish Chamber Orchestra and Irish Baroque Orchestra.

MfG's Artistic Director is acclaimed international pianist, Dubliner Finghin Collins.

Photo: Frances Marshall

MfG is grateful for the funding received by the Arts Council and Galway City Council, for the support from private and corporate sponsorship and for the goodwill of its many MfG Friends and Volunteers.

For information on the current season visit:

www.musicforgalway.ie

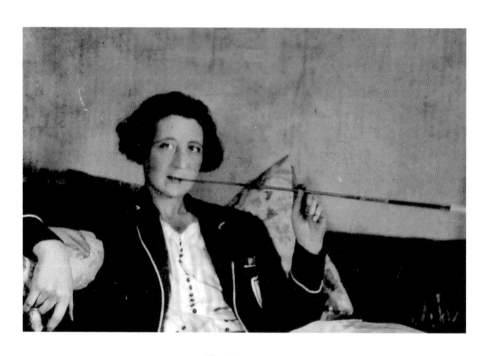

Poetry
by
Dell (Joyce) Allen

Beyond Those Hills

Beyond Maam Cross the friendly hills are waiting,
As sunset streaks the countryside with gold;
Westward we go into the heart of silence,
Children once more returning to the fold.
Beneath the wooded hills, Kylemore is silent,
Only the thrushes singing in the brake;
Here I have walked among the rhododendrons
And watched the shadows deepen on the lake.

So Many Things

From Muinterowen across the fields we raced,
Stopping for a moment by the hedge to taste
The wild, wet blackberries. So many things -
That bunch of primroses hidden in the lane,
That bearded goat who viewed us with distain.

Down from the hills the river swept in spate
Across the stepping-stones. Why should I hesitate,
When she was always there to rescue me,
To guide my feet from stone to stone
Until I had the confidence to cross alone?

Through Culliaghbeg we ran, through Thievnamong,
Over the stile we tumbled, breathless, flushed and young.
If we were late for school, she took the blame
And stood in brave defence of me.
Just as she did through all the years 'til yesterday...

The rowan trees trembled as the evening came,
The whispering river seemed to speak her name;
I saw again the seven stepping-stones
The wooded cliff, the ivied wall,
The curlew circled low - I heard his lonely call.

They Will Remember

Through crowded streets ablaze with festive lights
Lonely they'll walk in their adopted land
Dreaming of home and cherished days of youth
Like shipwrecked sailors on a foreign strand.

Will they perhaps recall some long lost tune
Once softly played within the firelight's glow,
Or see the flicker of a candle's gleam
On cobbled streets, footprinted in the snow?

Will they remember landmarks of their youth
Broad fields of wheat by roadsides in Kildare
A salmon leaping in a Galway lake
A blackbird whistling in a Dublin square?

Will they recall the Shannon at Athlone
The Kerry coast, peaks misty in the dawn
The Barrow and the Suir, the lovely Lee
The Wicklow hills in sheltered peace withdrawn?

Such pictures once were fresh in memory's frame
Until the veil of years was overcast;
But wistfully each one will to try to fill
Parts missing from the jig-saw of the past.

Around the hearth we'll gently speak their names,
And faces in the fire will slowly form;
May God be with them in each land they dwell
And keep them safe in sunshine and in storm.

Lost Leader

Your mighty task
Was yet a friendly task,
Discarding ancient precepts now outgrown;
Within the clutter of a tangled world
You strove to build an edifice of stone.

Your gifted hands
Were steady, guiding hands,
That gripped the rudder when the storm rode high
And, steering darkly towards the shore of peace,
You glimpsed the sunlight in tomorrow's sky.

Your simple words
Yet dedicated words
Gave sympathetic counsel or command;
With hope in you, and firm belief in you,
Men looked into the future that you planned.

Your far-seeing eyes
Were yet a dreamer's eyes
That saw the distant clouds suffused with light;
The darkness came - a moment's puzzlement
Before all things were blotted from your sight.

Like Wine

Where the river curved through the valley,
And ferns leaned forward to peep
Cautiously down at their lacy tips,
In pools that were still and deep,
Where spray from a waterfall spattered
In a grey mist silver-starred,
A boy was standing motionless
Like a sentinel on guard.

Had he seen or heard the Leprechaun
Who followed the cobbler's trade,
Or was he rapt in the melody
Of a blackbird's serenade?
Were his eager thoughts of adventure,
Dream castles building on air,
Incited by deeds of gallant men
The heroes who do and dare?

Then I saw the jar, chock-full of bait,
And the rod of crude design.
Had I forgotten the things that go
To a youthful head like wine -
That a chap must always concentrate
When a brown trout holds the line!

Connemara

The tangled heather blooms beside
Gorse bushes washed by summer rain,
As sunset dyes the waves with red,
Dark curraghs loom around the Head,
Oars creaking as the rowlocks strain.
The road curves inward by the sea,
Zigzagging on capriciously
But fuchsia blooms, by low stone walls,
Threading its way to Aasleagh Falls
Where Erriff flows to Killary.

What's My Line?

Tales of mystery and detection with a multitude of clues,
Lurid books in gaudy jackets such as *Murder in the Mews*:
Such has been my reading-matter - but indeed it's nearly time
That I aimed at something bigger and gave up this life of crime!

My neglected education is a fact I much deplore,
There are avenues of knowledge that I might well explore,
So I linger in the library and wonder what's my line;
I must organise my reading to follow some design.

Could I specialise in Classics and study for degrees?
Perhaps I'd find my métier in French or Portuguese?
Mythology? Astrology - the shape of things to be?
Geology? Biology? Psychology? *Not me*!

I seek among the bookshelves for something less obscure:
Political Economy I simply can't endure,
I feel no urge towards History, Biography, or Law,
I'd be addled by the genius of Shakespeare or of Shaw!

Then suddenly I make my choice and beat a quick retreat,
I hasten through the library and now I'm in the street;
Away with all this highbrow stuff! It's far beyond my range
I've picked another thriller - bound in yellow for a change!

Footprints

Someday I'll rest my head beside
the purple heather,
And slowly I'll retrace the footprints
Time has made;
Some will be clear and well-defined,
Some fresh as yesterday,
Some hesitant, uncertain, as of a
child who strayed.

Someday I'll take my rest beside
the purple heather,
And watch the distant peaks outlined
against the sky;
Before the darkness falls, I'll hear
the voice of childhood,
Within the lonely valley
Where no one passes by

(Poem read at Joyce funerals)

I have looked upon those brilliant creatures,
And now my heart is sore,
All's changed since I, hearing at twilight,
The first time on this shore,
The bell-beat of their wings above my head,
Trod with a lighter tread.

Unwearied still, lover by lover,
They paddle in the cold
Companionable streams or climb the air;
Their hearts have not grown old;
Passion or conquest, wander where they will,
Attend upon them still.

But now they drift on the still water,
Mysterious, beautiful;
Among what rushes will they build,
By what lake's edge or pool
Delight men's eyes when I awake some day
To find they have flown away?

('*The Wild Swans at Coole*', W.B. Yeats)

Photo Gallery

Family and Friends

Grandfather - Thomas Francis Joyce

Grandmother - Sabina (Conroy) Joyce

Francis Joyce with his young brother John (my father) in the back seat

John M. Joyce
First shipment of wool from Dublin to Italy

John M. Joyce
President of The Irish Wool Federation 1954

Wedding photograph
Right - Professor Conor O' Malley and Dr Sal (Joyce) O' Malley

Cousin - Dr Patrick O' Malley (son of Conor and Sal O' Malley)
and wife Imelda

My father's sisters (from left) Dell, Sal and Bina

John and Marty Joyce with daughters (from left)
Patricia, Ann and Margaret

From left - Nephew Sean Joyce, Arthur Joyce
and Stephen Allen, grandson of poet Dell (Joyce) Allen

Niece - Joyce Healy, her mother Margaret (Joyce) Brereton and daughter-in-law Grace Brereton

Joyce (Brereton) Healy and husband Gearóid

Sister - Mary Joyce

Patrick McGinley and son Joseph. Patrick enjoyed many summer
holidays with his grandparents, Michael
and Mary 'Missie' Hastings, in Leenane

David O'Reilly (right) Master of North Galway Hunt
The Lawn Meet - Lady Molly Cusack Smith, Bramham House, Tuam

Myriam O'Reilly and Joe Schmidt - Rugby Coach
for Ireland from 2013-2019

On the way to the Gresham Hotel for morning coffee
From left - Amelia with cousins Claire (Allen) McMyler and
Hilda (Allen) Furminger - daughters of poet Del (Joyce) Allen

Frank and Hilda (Allen) Furminger with son Michael

Cousin - Hugh O'Malley with Loretto,
Damien and Grace

Cousin - Joan (O'Malley) Ringrose with husband Colonel Billy Ringrose, one of Ireland's most successful show jumpers. He won the Grand Prix in Nice, presented by Princess Grace and in Rome, presented by Queen Elizabeth II who was on a State visit to Italy

Fashion designer Neillí Mulcahy with former models Liz (Willoughby) O'Rourke and Rosemarie (Scully) Mulcahy, modeling designs from her collection aboard the QE2 on our visit to the USA in 1967

Friend - Joe Skelton
Former Paratrooper with the French Foreign Legion

Amelia at the graveside of Sir Ernest Shackleton
Grytviken Cemetery, South Georgia Island
Headstone inscription: *I hold ... that a man should strive to the utmost*
for his life's set prize. (Robert Browning)

Friends - Patrick and Patricia Flood

Friend - Beatrice Lawless

Etta (Vaughan) O'Sullivan (on the right): stand-in for Maureen O'Hara

Amelia with friend Myriam O'Reilly

Bibliography

Allen, Dell, *Before the Rain Began* (Tortoise Press, 1975).

Behnam, William Gurney, *A Book of Quotations, Proverbs and Household Words* (Cassell & Co., 1907).

Burke, Ray, *Joyce County: Galway and James Joyce* (Curragh Press, 2016).

Chambers, Anne, *Granuaile: The Life and Times of Grace O' Malley, c. 1530-1603* (Wolfhound Press, 1998).

Chambers, Anne, *Ranji Maharajah of Connemara* (Wolfhound Press, 2002).

Chekhov, Anton P., 'A Day in the Country' in *The Lady with the Dog and Other Stories* (first published in 1899).

Ellmann, Richard, *Oscar Wilde – a collection of critical essays* (Prentice-Hall, 1969).

Gibbons, Michael, *Connemara - Visions of Iar Chonnacht* (Cottage Publications, 2004).

Gide, André P.G., 'Les faux-monnayeurs' ['The counterfeiters'] (first published in *Nouvelle Revue Francaise*, 1925).

Healey, Elizabeth, *Literary Tour of Ireland* (Wolfhound Press, 1995).

Inglis, Henry David, *A journey throughout Ireland during the Spring, Summer, and Autumn of 1834* (first published in 2 Volumes by Whittaker & Co, 1835).

Johnson, Joan C., *James and Mary Ellis: Background and Quaker Famine Relief in Letterfrack* (Historical Committee of the Religious Society of Friends in Ireland, 2000).

Kilroy, Patricia, *The Story of Connemara* (Gill and Macmillan, 1989).

Lynam, Shevawn, Humanity Dick Martin '*King of Connemara*' 1754-1834 (The Lilliput Press Ltd, 1989).

McLaren, Duncan, In Ruins - *The Once Great Houses of Ireland* (Little, Brown and Company Inc., 1997).

McNee, Gerry, *In the Footsteps of the Quiet Man – The Inside Story of the Cult Film* (Mainstream Publishing Company, 1990).

Morton, H.V., *In search of Ireland* (Methuen, 1930).

Robinson, Tim, *Connemara: A Little Gaelic Kingdom* (Penguin Ireland, 2011).

Villiers-Tuthill, Kathleen, *Beyond the Twelve Bens: A History of Clifden and District, 1860-1923* (K. Villiers-Tuthill, 1986).

Villiers-Tuthill, Kathleen, *History of Kylemore Castle & Abbey* (Kylemore Abbey Publications, 2002).

Whilde, Tony, *The Natural History of Connemara* (Immel Publishing, 1994).

Wilde, Oscar, *The Picture of Dorian Gray* (first published in *Lippincott's Monthly Magazine*, 1890).

Coyne, Joseph Sterling and Bartlett, William Henry., *The Scenery and Antiquities of Ireland* - (Published by George Virtue, London 1842).

Photography credits:
Gardiner Mitchell: pages ix,2,10/Tim Moran: p8/Des Glynn: Solas
Photo Club p34/Sean Tomkins: pages 30,48,56,65/ Michael Paul:
Conde Nast Traveller p54/Aoife Herriott: p61/Helene Brennan: p63/
Richard Murphy: p71/Alamy Stock Photos: Dennis Frates: p16/
David Robertson: p25/Chris Hill: p69/Martin Siepman: p50/Manfred
Grebler: p6/Steve Taylor: p73/Failte Ireland: p67/Pixels-Pierre Leclerc:
p46/Pixabay-Tommy Tau: p75/Back cover photo: Ashley Morrison

Courtesy Photographs:
Ballynainch Castle p38
Ashford Castle p20
Leenane Hotel p52
Renvyle Hotel p35

Painting: Page 41
Humanity Dick. Colonel Richard Martin, MP.
From the portrait hanging in the board room of the RSPCA in London

Joyce surname popularity worldwide:
Approx 96,700 bear the surname Joyce.
According to Forbes: Names & Genealogy Resources, the Joyce name is
the most occurring surname throughout the world - most prevalent in
the following countries:
USA - 47,500
England - 18,221
Australia - 8.400
Ireland - 6,532
Canada - 4,603
New Zealand - 2,450

Joyce Memorials

John 'Sean' Francis Joyce (1937-2017)

Margaret 'Marty' (Vaughan) Joyce (1913-1991)

John Martin Joyce (1907-1992)

Thomas 'Francis' Joyce (1899-1970)

Anna Rosaline 'Rosie' (Hastings) Joyce (1915-2009)

Sarah 'Sal' (Joyce) O'Malley (1896-1959)

Madeline 'Dell' (Joyce) Allen (1898-1985)

Thomas Francis Joyce (1853-1922)

Sabina (Conroy) Joyce (1870-1926)

Patrick Joyce (1814-1888)

Ann (O'Duffy) Joyce (1809-1900)

John 'Jack' Joyce (1786-1856)

Map
of
Journeys

Permit No. 9192

Ordnance
Survey

Ordnance Survey Ireland Permit No. 9192
© Ordnance Survey Ireland/Government of Ireland

OSi

103

Printed in Great Britain
by Amazon